TABLE OF CONTENTS

INTRODUCTION: FROM FEAR TO FLOURISHING

Everyone has a story to tell, a message to share, and a voice that deserves to be heard. But for many, the mere thought of standing in front of an audience, all eyes locked on them, is enough to send shivers down their spine. Their heart races, their palms sweat, and their mind fills with a torrent of self-doubt and panic. I know this feeling all too well because I, too, have struggled with the paralyzing fear of public speaking.

For over 14 years, I have served in the United States Air Force, working my way up through the ranks and taking on various roles that have tested my limits and pushed me out of my comfort zone. My journey has led me to manage ground transportation at Osan Air Base in South Korea, coordinate logistics for high-level peace talks, and supervise a team of 50 dedicated airmen. Yet, despite my accomplishments, I could not escape the specter of anxiety that haunted me every time I had to address a group of people.

When I transitioned into the role of a recruiter for the United States Air Force, public speaking became an essential part of my job. I had to face my fears and find ways to communicate effectively with potential recruits and influencers. But my anxiety was relentless, manifesting itself in a racing heart, uncontrollable sweating, and a deep, gnawing fear of judgment from others.

As I grappled with these challenges, I realized that I was not alone in my struggle. Public speaking anxiety is a common experience shared by millions of people worldwide. I knew that if I could find a way to overcome my own fears and become a more effective speaker, I could help countless others do the same. This quest for self-improvement led me to interview doctors, attend workshops, and voraciously consume books on public speaking and anxiety management.

It was during this time that I discovered the work of Tony Robbins, a world-renowned motivational speaker who has inspired millions of people to transform their lives. His charisma, passion, and powerful message resonated deeply with me, and I found myself turning to his teachings for guidance and inspiration. With each new technique I learned, I began to see glimpses of the confident and captivating speaker I longed to become.

This book is the culmination of my journey, a distillation of the insights, experiences, and wisdom I have gathered along the way. It is my hope that by sharing my story, I can provide you with the tools and encouragement you need to conquer your own fears and step into your power as a public speaker.

In the pages that follow, we will explore the science behind anxiety and public speaking, delving into the psychological and physiological processes that fuel our fears. We will examine strategies for preparing, practicing, and perfecting your speeches, as well as techniques for mastering your mindset and overcoming negative self-talk. Together, we will learn how to stay calm and collected under pressure, engage and captivate our audiences, and gracefully navigate the challenges and obstacles that arise during public speaking engagements.

As we embark on this journey together, I invite you to reflect on your own experiences, fears, and aspirations. This is not just a book about public speaking; it is a roadmap to self-discovery and personal growth. By confronting our fears and embracing our vulnerabilities, we can unlock our true potential and transform not only our public speaking abilities but also our lives.

As you read, I encourage you to keep an open mind and a curious spirit. Try new techniques, experiment with different approaches, and most importantly, be kind to yourself as you learn and grow. Remember that becoming a confident and effective public speaker is a process that takes time, patience, and perseverance. No one becomes an overnight sensation, but with dedication and the right guidance, you can make incredible strides in your journey.

One of the most powerful lessons I have learned is the importance of embracing failure as an opportunity for growth. As you work through the chapters of this book and apply the principles to your own life, remember that setbacks and mistakes are an inevitable part of the learning process. They are not signs of failure, but rather, valuable experiences from which we can gain wisdom and insight.

In addition to the practical tips and techniques, this book will also emphasize the importance of finding your unique voice and developing your personal style as a speaker. We are all different, and what works for one person may not resonate with another. By exploring your strengths, passions, and experiences, you can craft a message that is both authentic and compelling.

As we reach the conclusion of this book, I hope to inspire you to continue your journey and take your public speaking skills to new heights. Embrace the opportunities that come your way, seek out mentors and learning experiences, and never stop striving to improve.

Through the power of public speaking, we can create a ripple effect that touches the lives of countless people. Our words have the power to inspire, motivate, and transform, and by conquering our fears and stepping into our power, we can leave a lasting impact on the world.

So, let's embark on this journey together. Let's face our fears, embrace our vulnerabilities, and unlock the potential within each of us. Join me as we conquer the stage, transform our public speaking anxiety into confidence and power, and ultimately, change the world— one speech at a time.

Welcome to "Conquering the Stage." Your journey starts now.

CHAPTER 1: UNDERSTANDING YOUR ANXIETY

Section 1: The Science Behind Anxiety and Public Speaking

Anxiety is a natural, biological response to perceived threats or stressors. It is a survival mechanism that has evolved over time to help us respond to danger. When we perceive a threat, our brain's amygdala activates the fight-or-flight response, releasing stress hormones like adrenaline and cortisol. These hormones prepare our body for action, increasing our heart rate, blood pressure, and breathing rate.

Public speaking anxiety, also known as glossophobia, is a common form of social anxiety. It occurs when we fear being judged, humiliated, or rejected while speaking in front of others. This fear can be so intense that it interferes with our ability to perform, causing physical symptoms like trembling, sweating, and a racing heart.

Research suggests that public speaking anxiety is rooted in our evolutionary history. In early human societies, social acceptance and group cohesion were crucial for survival. Being ostracized or rejected by the group could result in death. As a result, our brains have evolved to be acutely sensitive to social threats, making us susceptible to anxiety in situations where we feel exposed or vulnerable, like public speaking.

Section 2: Identifying Your Triggers: What Makes You Nervous

To overcome public speaking anxiety, it's essential to identify the specific triggers that cause you to feel nervous or fearful. Triggers can be different for everyone and may include:

1. Fear of judgment or criticism: Worries about being judged, criticized, or rejected can fuel public speaking anxiety. This fear

can stem from past experiences or a lack of confidence in our abilities.

2. Lack of preparation: Feeling unprepared or underprepared can make us feel more vulnerable and anxious. This can be due to a lack of time, resources, or knowledge about the subject matter.

3. High-stakes situations: High-pressure situations, such as job interviews, presentations to executives, or speeches in front of large audiences, can amplify anxiety levels.

4. Unfamiliar environments: Speaking in new or unfamiliar settings can increase anxiety because it adds an element of uncertainty.

5. Negative self-talk: Negative thoughts about ourselves, our abilities, or the situation can exacerbate anxiety and create a self-fulfilling prophecy.

To identify your triggers, take the time to reflect on past public speaking experiences that have caused you anxiety. Consider keeping a journal to track your feelings and thoughts before, during, and after speaking engagements. This can help you uncover patterns and pinpoint the specific triggers that contribute to your anxiety.

Section 3: The Mind-Body Connection: How Your Thoughts Affect Your Physical Reactions

The mind and body are intricately connected, and our thoughts can have a profound impact on our physical reactions. In the context of public speaking anxiety, negative thoughts and beliefs can trigger the body's stress response, leading to symptoms like a racing heart, shallow breathing, and muscle tension.

To manage these physical reactions, it's essential to address the underlying thoughts and beliefs that fuel them. Cognitive-behavioral techniques can be effective in changing negative thought patterns and reducing anxiety. These strategies include:

1. Cognitive restructuring: This technique involves identifying and challenging irrational thoughts and beliefs related to

public speaking. By replacing these thoughts with more balanced, rational alternatives, you can reduce anxiety and improve your performance.

2. Mindfulness and acceptance: Practicing mindfulness can help you become more aware of your thoughts, feelings, and bodily sensations without judgment. Acceptance involves acknowledging your anxiety and allowing it to be present without trying to suppress or control it. This can help you create distance from your anxiety and reduce its intensity.

3. Exposure therapy: Gradually facing your fears through repeated exposure to public speaking situations can help desensitize you to the anxiety-provoking triggers. Start with low-stakes situations and work your way up to more challenging ones. This process helps build confidence and resilience over time.

4. Visualization and mental rehearsal: Imagining yourself successfully delivering a speech or presentation can help train your

brain to remain calm and focused in real-life situations. By mentally rehearsing your performance, you can create positive associations with public speaking and reduce anxiety.

5. Affirmations and self-compassion: Positive affirmations can help counteract negative self-talk and boost self-confidence. Practice self-compassion by acknowledging that it's normal to feel anxious and that you're doing your best to face your fears and improve.

By addressing the thoughts and beliefs that contribute to public speaking anxiety, you can better manage the physical reactions that accompany it. Remember that the mind-body connection is a powerful tool in overcoming anxiety and improving your public speaking performance.

Understanding the science behind anxiety and public speaking, identifying your triggers, and learning how your thoughts affect your physical reactions are crucial steps in overcoming public speaking anxiety. By gaining insight into these aspects of your anxiety, you'll be better equipped to face your fears, develop effective coping strategies, and ultimately transform your anxiety into confidence and power.

CHAPTER 2: PREPARING FOR SUCCESS

Section 1: Research and Planning: Laying the Foundation

A strong foundation is essential for a successful public speaking performance. To lay this foundation, invest time in researching your topic and planning your speech. This process involves gathering relevant information, analyzing your audience, and determining your goals and objectives.

First, start by gathering information about your topic from reliable sources. This can include books, articles, studies, and expert interviews. As you gather information, take notes and keep track of your sources for later reference. This research phase will not only make you more knowledgeable about your topic but also give you the confidence to speak with authority.

Next, analyze your audience to understand their needs, interests, and expectations. Consider factors such as age, education level, cultural background, and prior knowledge of the subject matter. By tailoring your speech to your audience, you can make it more engaging and relevant.

Finally, set clear goals and objectives for your speech. What do you want your audience to learn, feel, or do as a result of your presentation? Establishing a clear purpose can help you stay focused and ensure that your message is both cohesive and compelling.

Section 2: Structuring Your Speech: Crafting a Compelling Message

A well-structured speech is essential for effectively conveying your message and maintaining your audience's attention. A compelling speech typically includes an introduction, body, and conclusion.

1. Introduction: The purpose of the introduction is to grab the audience's attention, establish credibility, and set the tone for your speech. Begin with a strong opening that engages your audience, such as a quote, anecdote, or surprising fact. Then, introduce yourself and briefly outline your speech's main points.

2. Body: The body of your speech should be organized around your main points, which should be supported by evidence, examples, and explanations. Use clear transitions between points to help your audience follow your train of thought. To make your speech more engaging, incorporate storytelling, metaphors, and analogies that help illustrate your points and connect with your audience on an emotional level.

3. Conclusion: The conclusion should summarize your main points and reiterate your speech's purpose. End with a strong closing statement that leaves a lasting impression on your audience. This could be

a call to action, a memorable quote, or a thought-provoking question.

When structuring your speech, consider using techniques such as the rule of three, which suggests that information presented in groups of three is more memorable and impactful. Additionally, be mindful of your speech's pacing, avoiding lengthy sections that may cause your audience to lose interest.

Section 3: Rehearsal: The Key to Confidence

Rehearsing your speech is crucial for building confidence and refining your delivery. Through rehearsal, you can identify and address any weaknesses, become more familiar with your material, and develop a natural, engaging speaking style.

1. Practice out loud: Rehearsing your speech out loud allows you to get a feel for the pacing, tone, and flow of your presentation.

It also helps you identify areas that need improvement, such as awkward phrasing or confusing transitions.

2. Use a timer: Time your rehearsals to ensure that your speech fits within the allotted time frame. This will help you avoid rushing or running out of time during your actual presentation.

3. Record yourself: Recording your rehearsals can provide valuable insights into your body language, facial expressions, and vocal delivery. Review your recordings to identify areas for improvement and track your progress.

4. Rehearse in front of others: Practicing your speech in front of a supportive audience, such as friends or family members, can help you become more comfortable with public speaking and receive valuable feedback.

5. Visualize success: Before and during your rehearsals, visualize yourself delivering a successful, engaging speech. This mental exercise can help build your confidence and

prepare your mind for a successful performance.

6. Practice under varying conditions: Rehearse in different settings and situations to become more adaptable and comfortable with the unexpected. This could include practicing in a noisy environment or using different types of microphones or audiovisual equipment.

7. Rehearse your transitions and pauses: Effective transitions and pauses are essential for maintaining your audience's attention and ensuring that your speech flows smoothly. Practice incorporating these elements into your speech to make your delivery more polished and professional.

By rehearsing your speech thoroughly, you'll not only build confidence but also fine-tune your delivery and presentation skills. Remember that practice makes progress, and the more you rehearse, the more comfortable and effective you'll become as a public speaker.

Preparing for success in public speaking involves thorough research and planning, crafting a compelling and well-structured message, and dedicated rehearsal. By investing time and effort into these key areas, you'll be well-equipped to deliver an engaging, impactful speech that leaves a lasting impression on your audience. Embrace the preparation process as an opportunity for growth and self-improvement, and remember that with each speech, you're building the skills and confidence needed to excel in public speaking.

CHAPTER 3: MASTERING YOUR MINDSET

Section 1: Visualization Techniques: Seeing Yourself Succeed

Visualization is a powerful technique that can help you mentally prepare for public speaking engagements and improve your performance. By creating vivid mental images of yourself delivering a successful speech, you train your mind to associate public speaking with positive outcomes, ultimately increasing your self-confidence.

To practice visualization:

1. Find a quiet, comfortable space where you can relax and focus.
2. Close your eyes and take several deep breaths, allowing your body to relax.

3. Imagine yourself in the setting of your upcoming speech, including specific details such as the size of the room, the arrangement of the seating, and the appearance of the audience.
4. Envision yourself confidently walking up to the stage or podium, feeling calm and prepared.
5. Mentally rehearse your speech, imagining the sound of your voice, your body language, and your facial expressions. Visualize your audience reacting positively, nodding in agreement, and applauding your points.
6. As you conclude your speech, imagine receiving enthusiastic applause and praise from the audience.
7. Take a few more deep breaths, and when you're ready, open your eyes.

Repeat this visualization exercise regularly, especially in the days leading up to your speech. The more vivid and realistic your mental images, the more effective this technique will be in boosting your confidence and improving your performance.

Section 2: Affirmations and Self-Talk: Becoming Your Own Cheerleader

Positive affirmations and self-talk can be powerful tools for overcoming public speaking anxiety and building self-confidence. By replacing negative thoughts with positive, empowering statements, you can retrain your brain to view public speaking as an opportunity rather than a threat.

To incorporate positive affirmations and self-talk into your preparation:

1. Identify common negative thoughts that arise during public speaking, such as "I'll mess up" or "They'll think I'm stupid."
2. Create positive affirmations that counteract these negative thoughts, such as "I am well-prepared and confident" or "I have valuable insights to share."
3. Repeat your affirmations regularly, especially when negative thoughts arise.

Say them out loud, write them down, or display them in a visible location.

4. Practice self-compassion by acknowledging that it's normal to feel nervous and that you're doing your best to face your fears and improve.
5. Remember past successes and use them as evidence to support your positive self-talk.
6. Encourage yourself with statements like "I can do this" and "I am capable."

By consistently practicing positive affirmations and self-talk, you can shift your mindset and develop a more optimistic, confident approach to public speaking.

Section 3: Embracing Failure: Learning from Your Mistakes

No public speaker is perfect, and everyone makes mistakes from time to time. Rather than fearing failure, embrace it as a valuable learning opportunity that can help you grow and improve as a speaker.

To learn from your mistakes:

1. Reflect on past speaking experiences, both successful and unsuccessful. Identify areas where you struggled or could have done better.

2. Analyze what went wrong and determine what you can do differently in the future. This may involve refining your speech content, improving your delivery, or adopting new coping strategies for anxiety.

3. Develop a plan of action for addressing your weaknesses and incorporating your newfound insights into future speeches.

4. Practice self-forgiveness and accept that mistakes are a natural part of the learning process. Let go of any lingering feelings of shame or embarrassment and focus on your growth and progress.

5. Remember that even the most accomplished speakers have faced setbacks and failures. Use their stories as inspiration and motivation to continue improving.

By embracing failure and viewing it as an opportunity for growth and learning, you can develop a more resilient mindset that will serve you well in your public speaking journey.

In conclusion, mastering your mindset is crucial for overcoming public speaking anxiety and achieving success. By practicing visualization techniques, engaging in positive affirmations and self-talk, and embracing failure as a learning opportunity, you can transform your mental approach to public speaking and become a more confident, capable speaker. Remember that your mindset plays a significant role in your performance, and by cultivating a positive, growth-oriented mindset, you'll be well-equipped to face the challenges of public speaking and emerge victorious.

CHAPTER 4: TECHNIQUES FOR STAYING CALM AND COLLECTED

Section 1: Breathing Exercises: Regaining Control in Stressful Situations

Breathing exercises can be a powerful tool for calming your nerves and regaining control in stressful situations, such as public speaking engagements. By focusing on your breath, you can help slow your heart rate, reduce anxiety, and improve focus.

Here are some effective breathing exercises to try:

1. Diaphragmatic breathing: Also known as belly breathing, diaphragmatic breathing involves inhaling deeply through your nose, allowing your diaphragm to expand and fill your lungs with air. As you exhale through your mouth, contract your diaphragm to push the air out. Practice this technique for several minutes, focusing on the rise and fall of your abdomen.

2. 4-7-8 breathing: Inhale through your nose for a count of four, hold your breath for a count of seven, and then exhale through your mouth for a count of eight. Repeat this cycle several times, concentrating on maintaining a steady rhythm.

3. Box breathing: Inhale for a count of four, hold your breath for a count of four, exhale for a count of four, and then hold your breath again for a count of four. Repeat this pattern several times, visualizing a box as you complete each cycle.

Practice these breathing exercises regularly, especially in the days leading up to your speech, and use them as needed during your presentation to help maintain calm and composure.

Section 2: Mindfulness and Meditation: Cultivating Inner Peace

Mindfulness and meditation can help you cultivate inner peace and improve your ability to manage stress and anxiety associated with public speaking. By practicing mindfulness, you learn to observe your thoughts and feelings nonjudgmentally, allowing you to better regulate your emotions and maintain focus during your speech.

Here are some mindfulness and meditation techniques to try:

1. Body scan meditation: Find a comfortable position and take several deep breaths. Starting at the top of your head and working your way down to your toes, bring your attention to each part of your body, noting any sensations or tension. As you focus on each area, imagine releasing any tension and relaxing your muscles.

2. Mindful breathing: Sit or lie down in a comfortable position and focus your attention on your breath. Observe each inhale and exhale without trying to change or control your breathing. If your mind wanders, gently bring your focus back to your breath.

3. Loving-kindness meditation: Begin by focusing on your breath and silently repeating phrases such as "May I be happy, may I be healthy, may I be safe, may I be at ease." Gradually expand your focus to include others, such as loved ones, acquaintances, and even those you may have difficulty with, repeating the phrases for each person.

Incorporate mindfulness and meditation practices into your daily routine to help build resilience, improve emotional regulation, and enhance your overall well-being.

Section 3: The Power of Perspective: Shifting Your Focus from Fear to Excitement

One key to staying calm and collected during public speaking engagements is to shift your perspective from fear to excitement. By viewing your speech as an opportunity to share your knowledge, inspire others, or make a positive impact, you can transform your anxiety into enthusiasm and motivation.

Here are some strategies for shifting your perspective:

1. Reframe your thoughts: Instead of thinking, "I'm terrified of speaking in front of this audience," tell yourself, "I'm excited to share my message with these people."
2. Focus on the benefits: Remind yourself of the potential positive outcomes of your speech, such as personal growth, increased credibility, or the chance to make a difference in the lives of your listeners.

3. Embrace the adrenaline: Recognize that the physical sensations associated with anxiety, such as a racing heart or butterflies in your stomach, can also be signs of excitement. Reframe these sensations as evidence that you're energized and ready to perform.

4. Visualize success: Instead of dwelling on potential negative outcomes, imagine yourself delivering a captivating, successful speech. Envision the audience reacting positively and applauding your efforts.

5. Adopt a growth mindset: View each public speaking opportunity as a chance to learn, grow, and improve your skills. Embrace challenges and focus on the progress you're making rather than striving for perfection.

By shifting your perspective from fear to excitement, you can approach public speaking engagements with a sense of enthusiasm and anticipation rather than dread. This change in mindset can have a profound impact on your ability to stay calm, focused, and collected during your speech.

Finally, staying calm and collected during public speaking engagements is essential for delivering a successful, engaging speech. By incorporating breathing exercises, mindfulness and meditation practices, and shifting your perspective from fear to excitement, you can cultivate the inner peace and composure necessary to excel in public speaking. Remember that managing anxiety is an ongoing process, and by consistently practicing these techniques, you'll build the resilience and mental fortitude needed to thrive as a public speaker.

CHAPTER 5: ENGAGING YOUR AUDIENCE

Section 1: Body Language: The Silent Language of Confidence

Body language is a powerful, often overlooked aspect of public speaking that can significantly impact your audience's perception of you and your message. By mastering confident, engaging body language, you can create a positive impression and enhance the effectiveness of your speech.

Here are some key aspects of body language to consider:

1. Posture: Stand tall with your shoulders back and your head held high. This stance communicates confidence and helps you project your voice more effectively.

2. Eye contact: Maintain eye contact with your audience to create a connection and demonstrate that you're genuinely interested in their reactions. Try to distribute your eye contact evenly across the room, avoiding the temptation to focus on a single person or area.

3. Gestures: Use your hands and arms to emphasize your points and convey enthusiasm for your topic. Avoid excessive or repetitive gestures, which can be distracting, and strive for natural, expressive movements.
4. Facial expressions: Show genuine emotion and interest in your subject matter through your facial expressions. Smile when appropriate, and let your passion for your topic shine through.
5. Movement: Utilize the space available to you by moving around the stage or speaking area. This movement can help maintain audience engagement and prevent your speech from becoming static.

Practice and refine your body language during rehearsal, and consider recording yourself to identify areas for improvement. With practice, you can develop body language that projects confidence, competence, and genuine engagement with your audience.

Section 2: The Art of Storytelling: Connecting with Your Audience on a Personal Level

Storytelling is a powerful tool for connecting with your audience on a personal level, making your message more memorable and impactful. By incorporating anecdotes, personal experiences, or illustrative examples, you can create an emotional connection with your listeners and bring your message to life.

Here are some tips for effective storytelling in public speaking:

1. Choose stories that are relevant to your topic and support your key points. Ensure that your story has a clear purpose and adds value to your speech.
2. Keep your stories concise and focused, avoiding unnecessary details that may cause your audience to lose interest.
3. Use vivid language and descriptive details to paint a picture in your audience's mind, helping them to visualize and empathize with your experiences.
4. Practice your storytelling skills by rehearsing your anecdotes and refining your delivery to maximize impact.
5. Be authentic and genuine in your storytelling, sharing your emotions and personal insights to create a deeper connection with your audience.

By mastering the art of storytelling, you can make your public speaking engagements more engaging, memorable, and emotionally resonant for your audience.

Section 3: Active Listening and Responding: Building Rapport and Trust

Active listening and responding are essential skills for building rapport and trust with your audience during public speaking engagements. By demonstrating that you value your audience's input and are genuinely interested in their thoughts and opinions, you can create a more interactive, engaging experience.

Here are some strategies for active listening and responding during public speaking:

1. Encourage audience participation: Invite your audience to ask questions, share their thoughts, or participate in discussions throughout your speech. This engagement can help create a more dynamic, collaborative atmosphere.
2. Be present and attentive: Focus on your audience's comments and questions, giving them your full attention and avoiding distractions.
3. Reflect and paraphrase: Demonstrate your understanding of your audience's input by

reflecting their statements or paraphrasing their questions before responding.

4. Respond thoughtfully and respectfully: Address your audience's comments and questions with care, providing thoughtful, well-considered answers that demonstrate your expertise and respect for their perspectives.

5. Adapt your speech based on audience feedback: Be prepared to adjust your content or delivery based on audience feedback or reactions. Demonstrating flexibility and responsiveness to your audience's needs can help build rapport and trust.

By practicing active listening and responding during your public speaking engagements, you can create a more interactive, engaging experience for your audience, fostering a sense of rapport and trust that enhances the impact of your message.

Futhermore, engaging your audience is a critical aspect of successful public speaking. By mastering confident body language, honing your storytelling skills, and actively listening and responding to your audience's input, you can create a more dynamic, memorable, and impactful speaking experience. Remember that public speaking is not just about delivering information; it's about connecting with your audience on a personal level and leaving a lasting impression. By focusing on audience engagement, you'll be well on your way to becoming a more effective, captivating public speaker.

CHAPTER 6: OVERCOMING OBSTACLES AND CHALLENGES

Section 1: Handling Difficult Questions and Interruptions

Public speaking engagements often involve fielding questions and addressing interruptions from the audience. Learning how to handle these situations gracefully and effectively is essential for maintaining your composure and credibility during your speech.

Here are some strategies for managing difficult questions and interruptions:

1. Anticipate potential questions: Before your speech, consider what questions or concerns your audience may have and prepare thoughtful, well-researched responses. This preparation can help you feel more confident and in control during the Q&A portion of your presentation.

2. Stay composed and professional: If you're interrupted or faced with a challenging question, remain calm and poised. Take a moment to collect your thoughts before responding and maintain a respectful, professional demeanor.

3. Don't be afraid to admit when you don't know the answer: If you're unsure of how to respond to a question, it's better to admit your uncertainty than to provide an inaccurate or misleading answer. Let the audience member know that you'll look into their question and get back to them later, or direct them to a resource that may have the information they're seeking.

4. Address the question, but stay on track: While it's important to address your audience's concerns, be mindful of your speech's overall structure and flow. Briefly address the question or interruption, then smoothly transition back to your main points.

5. Establish ground rules: At the beginning of your speech, let your audience know how and when they can ask questions or provide input. Setting expectations upfront can help minimize interruptions and maintain a more structured, focused presentation.

By honing your ability to handle difficult questions and interruptions, you can ensure that your public speaking engagements remain engaging, informative, and on track.

Section 2: Embracing the Unexpected: How to Adapt When Things Don't Go as Planned

Public speaking engagements rarely go exactly as planned. From technical issues to last-minute changes in content, you may encounter a variety of unexpected challenges during your speech. Learning how to adapt and think on your feet is essential for maintaining your composure and delivering a successful presentation despite any obstacles.

Here are some tips for embracing the unexpected during public speaking:

1. Remain calm and composed: When faced with an unexpected challenge, take a deep breath and remind yourself that you're well-prepared and capable of handling the situation.

2. Be flexible and adaptable: Be willing to adjust your content, delivery, or timing as needed to accommodate unforeseen circumstances. This adaptability can help you maintain your credibility and professionalism, even when things don't go as planned.

3. Have a backup plan: Before your speech, consider potential challenges and develop contingency plans for addressing them. For example, if you're relying on technology for your presentation, have a backup copy of your materials on a separate device or in a printed format.

4. Use humor to diffuse tension: If appropriate, use humor to acknowledge and diffuse any tension or awkwardness created by unexpected challenges.

This lightheartedness can help put your audience at ease and maintain a positive atmosphere.

5. Learn from your experiences: After your speech, take time to reflect on the unexpected challenges you encountered and how you handled them. Use these experiences to inform your preparation and strategies for future public speaking engagements.

By embracing the unexpected and learning to adapt when things don't go as planned, you can develop the resilience and resourcefulness necessary to succeed as a public speaker, regardless of the circumstances.

Section 3: Dealing with Criticism and Feedback: Growing from Constructive Comments

As a public speaker, you'll inevitably encounter criticism and feedback from your audience. Learning how to handle these comments constructively and use them as opportunities for growth is essential for refining your skills and becoming a more effective communicator.

Here are some strategies for dealing with criticism and feedback:

Listen carefully and objectively: When faced with criticism, it's essential to listen carefully and objectively, without becoming defensive or dismissive. This open-mindedness can help you identify areas for improvement and demonstrate your commitment to growth.

Distinguish between constructive and unhelpful criticism: Not all feedback is equally valuable. Learn to discern between constructive criticism that provides actionable insights and unhelpful comments that are based on personal preferences or biases.

Ask for clarification: If you're unsure of the intent or meaning behind a piece of feedback, ask for clarification or examples to help you better understand the issue and how you can address it.

Reflect on the feedback: Take time after your speech to reflect on the feedback you received, considering how it aligns with your goals and values as a speaker. Use this reflection to inform your strategies and preparation for future engagements.

Develop an action plan for improvement: Based on the feedback you receive, develop a plan for addressing your areas of weakness and refining your skills. This proactive approach can help you become a more confident, effective public speaker over time.

Practice self-compassion: Remember that nobody is perfect, and every public speaker experiences setbacks and criticism. Treat yourself with kindness and compassion as you navigate the learning process, acknowledging that growth and improvement take time and effort.

By learning to handle criticism and feedback constructively, you can use these insights to grow and develop as a public speaker. Embrace the opportunity to learn from your audience and continuously refine your skills, recognizing that becoming a masterful communicator is an ongoing journey.

Overcoming obstacles and challenges is a vital aspect of successful public speaking. By mastering strategies for handling difficult questions, embracing the unexpected, and learning from criticism and feedback, you can develop the resilience, adaptability, and growth mindset necessary to excel in the dynamic world of public speaking. As you encounter and overcome these challenges, you'll gain valuable experience and insight that will help you become a more confident, effective, and engaging speaker.

CHAPTER 7: THE LONG-TERM JOURNEY: CONTINUOUS IMPROVEMENT

Section 1: Setting Goals and Tracking Progress

The journey toward becoming an exceptional public speaker is ongoing, and setting goals can help you stay focused on your growth and development. By establishing clear, measurable objectives, you can monitor your progress and celebrate your achievements along the way.

Here are some tips for setting goals and tracking progress in your public speaking journey:

Start by assessing your current abilities: Take an honest inventory of your current public speaking skills and identify the areas where you'd like to improve. This self-assessment can serve as a baseline for measuring your progress over time.

Set specific, achievable goals: Break down your overarching goal of becoming a better public speaker into smaller, manageable objectives. Ensure that your goals are specific, measurable, achievable, relevant, and time-bound (SMART).

Create a plan of action: Develop a step-by-step plan for achieving your goals, including the strategies, resources, and timeline you'll need to reach your objectives.

Monitor your progress: Regularly evaluate your progress toward your goals, reflecting on your successes and setbacks. Adjust your plan as needed to stay on track and maintain momentum.

Celebrate your achievements: As you reach milestones in your public speaking journey, take time to acknowledge and celebrate your accomplishments. These moments of recognition can help boost your motivation and confidence, fueling your continued growth.

By setting goals and tracking your progress, you can maintain focus on your long-term vision and ensure that you're continually moving forward in your public speaking journey.

Section 2: Finding Your Unique Voice: Developing a Personal Style

Each public speaker has a unique voice and style that sets them apart from others. Embracing and developing your personal style can help you connect more deeply with your audience and make a lasting impact with your message.

Here are some strategies for finding and refining your unique voice:

Reflect on your strengths and passions: Consider what sets you apart as a speaker and what you're most passionate about. Identifying your strengths and areas of interest can help you cultivate a speaking style that feels authentic and engaging.

Experiment with different approaches: Don't be afraid to try out different speaking techniques, delivery styles, or presentation formats. Experimenting with various approaches can help you discover what works best for you and your audience.

Seek feedback from trusted sources: Solicit feedback from friends, colleagues, or mentors who can provide honest, constructive insights into your speaking style. Use this feedback to refine your approach and further develop your unique voice.

Watch and learn from other speakers: Observe the speaking styles of others, both within and outside of your field. Take note of the techniques and approaches that resonate with you, and consider how you might incorporate these elements into your own style.

Continually refine and evolve: Your speaking style will likely evolve over time as you gain experience, learn from others, and grow in your abilities. Embrace this process of change and be open to continually refining your unique voice.

By developing a personal speaking style that reflects your strengths, passions, and experiences, you can create a more memorable, impactful connection with your audience.

Section 3: Never Stop Learning: The Value of Mentorship and Continuing Education

As with any skill, becoming a masterful public speaker requires ongoing learning and growth. Pursuing mentorship and continuing education opportunities can help you stay current on best practices, refine your skills, and expand your knowledge.

Here are some ways to embrace lifelong learning in your public speaking journey:

Seek out mentors and role models: Find experienced speakers who can provide guidance, advice, and support as you navigate your public speaking journey. Establishing mentorship relationships can help you learn from others' experiences and gain valuable insights into your own development.

Attend workshops and conferences: Participate in public speaking workshops, conferences, and other educational events to learn new techniques, network with other speakers, and stay current on industry trends.

Take courses or pursue certifications: Consider enrolling in public speaking courses or pursuing relevant certifications to deepen your knowledge and expertise. These structured learning opportunities can provide you with a solid foundation in the principles and best practices of effective communication.

Join professional organizations and clubs: Become a member of public speaking organizations or clubs, such as Toastmasters International, where you can practice your skills, receive feedback, and learn from others in a supportive environment.

Stay informed about new research and developments: Regularly read articles, books, and other resources on public speaking and communication to stay informed about the latest research, strategies, and tools in the field.

Learn from your own experiences: Reflect on your speaking engagements and use your successes and setbacks as learning opportunities. Analyze what worked well, what didn't, and how you can improve in future presentations.

Be open to feedback and constructive criticism: Embrace feedback from your audience, mentors, and peers as valuable learning opportunities. Use constructive criticism to identify areas for improvement and refine your skills over time.

By committing to ongoing learning and growth, you can ensure that you're always sharpening your public speaking abilities and staying at the forefront of best practices in the field.

The journey toward becoming a powerful, effective public speaker is a long-term commitment that requires continuous improvement, self-reflection, and perseverance. By setting goals, tracking your progress, and embracing lifelong learning, you can steadily refine your skills and develop a unique voice that resonates with your audience. Through mentorship, continuing education, and a willingness to learn from your experiences, you can achieve mastery in public speaking and make a lasting impact with your message. Remember, the key to success is to never stop learning and always strive to become a better version of yourself as a speaker and communicator.